# Henry Ford

### By Wil Mara

**Consultant**
Jeanne Clidas, Ph.D.
National Reading Consultant
and
Professor of Reading, SUNY Brockport

**ⴲ Children's Press ®**
A Division of Scholastic Inc.
New York  Toronto  London  Auckland  Sydney
Mexico City  New Delhi  Hong Kong
Danbury, Connecticut

Designer: Herman Adler Design
Photo Researcher: Caroline Anderson
The photo on the cover shows Henry Ford.

**Library of Congress Cataloging-in-Publication Data**

Mara, Wil.
  Henry Ford / by Wil Mara.
    p. cm. — (Rookie biographies)
Includes index.
  ISBN 0-516-25863-X (lib. bdg.)        0-516-27917-3 (pbk.)
  1. Ford, Henry, 1863-1947—Juvenile literature. 2. Industrialists—United
States—Biography—Juvenile literature. 3. Automobile industry and
trade—United States—Biography—Juvenile literature. 4. Automobile
engineers—United States—Biography—Juvenile literature. I. Title. II. Series:
Rookie biography.
  TL140.F6M325 2003
  338.7'6292'092-dc21

                    2003004588

CHILDREN'S PRESS, and ROOKIE BIOGRAPHIES™, and associated
logos are trademarks and or registered trademarks of Scholastic Library
Publishing. SCHOLASTIC and associated logos are trademarks and or
registered trademarks of Scholastic Inc.
4 5 6 7 8 9 10 R 12 11 10 09                62

Do you like to ride in cars?

4

Henry Ford invented the first modern car.

To "invent" something means to be the first person to create it.

He was born in Michigan
on July 30, 1863.

His father wanted him to be
a farmer when he grew up.

Ford did not like farm work. He was more interested in machines (muh-SHEENS).

A lawn mower is a machine.

Detroit

Ford went to Detroit, Michigan, when he was sixteen. He got a job fixing and building machines there.

Ford loved engines (EN-juhns).
Engines are what make many
machines work.

Farm tractor

Ships, trains, and farm
tractors could not run
without their engines.

A long time ago, people went from place to place in a carriage (KA-rij).

A carriage was like a big chair with wheels on it. It was pulled by horses.

15

16

Ford wanted to build a carriage that used an engine, instead of a horse. He worked on it in a shed behind his house.

In 1896, he built his first car.
He called it a quadricycle
(KWAHD-ruh-SYE-kuhl)
because it had four bicycle wheels.

It also had a doorbell for a horn!

FIRST · CAR

19

For many years, only rich people could buy cars.

Ford did not like this. He wanted everyone to have a car.

In 1903, Ford started
his own company.

Later that year, he built another car. He called it the Model A. He made sure it did not cost a lot of money.

Then he built another car.
He called it the Model T.

He sold millions (MIL-yuhnz)
of Model Ts. People called them
"Tin Lizzies."

To make more Model Ts,
Ford set up assembly
(uh-SEM-blee) lines.

Workers stood in one place.
Each time a car passed, a worker
would add a part. Cars were
made faster and cheaper.

Ford died in 1947.

If it weren't for him, we might
still be riding around in
carriages pulled by horses!

# Words You Know

assembly line

carriage

engine

Henry Ford

machine

Model A

quadricycle

Tin Lizzie

# Index

# About the Author

More than fifty published books bear Wil Mara's name. He has written both fiction and nonfiction, for both children and adults. He lives with his family in northern New Jersey.

# Photo Credits